Growing Up Right

Growing Up Right

A Child's Guide to Fundamental Duties

As Per NEP 2020 Guidelines

Abhishek Rana
Saumya

Published by
Renu Kaul Verma
Vitasta Publishing Pvt Ltd
4348/4C, Ansari Road, Daryaganj
New Delhi - 110 002

 an imprint of Vitasta Publishing

ISBN: 978-81-19670-29-1
© Vitasta Publishing Pvt Ltd
First Edition 2025
MRP ₹ 350

All Rights Reserved.
No part of this publication may be reproduced, stored in a retrieval system, or transmitted in any form, or by any means—electronic, mechanical, photocopying, recording or otherwise—without the prior permission of the publisher. The information provided in this book is for educational and informational purposes only. While efforts have been made to ensure accuracy, this book does not serve as substitute for official constitutional texts.

Book Design by Rohit Gautam
Printed by Chaman Enterprises, New Delhi

CONTENTS

Publisher's Note	1
Preamble	3
A Trip to Kartavya Path	4
Fundamental Duty 1: Pride in Our National Flag	12
Activity: National Symbol Explorer	14
Fundamental Duty 2: The Freedom Struggle	17
Activity: Time Travel Mission	20
Fundamental Duty 3: Public Property Belongs to all of Us	23
Activity: Guardians of Public Spaces	27
Fundamental Duty 4: Preserve the Unity of Our Nation	30
Activity: Unity is Powerful	33
Fundamental Duty 5: Our National Heritage	35
Activity: Guardians of Our National Heritage!	37
Fundamental Duty 6: Develop a Spirit of Inquiry	40
Activity: Be a Curious Explorer!	42

Fundamental Duty 7: Right to Education — 44
Activity: Education is My Superpower! — 48

Fundamental Duty 8: This Earth Belongs to all of Us — 50
Activity: You are a Guardian of the Earth! — 53

Fundamental Duty 9: Let Our Country be a Centre of Excellence — 56
Activity: My Path to Excellence — 58

Fundamental Duty 10: Everyone is Equal, Respect One-another — 60
Activity: We are all Special! — 64

Fundamental Duty 11: Safeguard Our Nation — 66
Activity: The Nation's Helper Detective — 71

Beyond Fundamental Duties — 73

- How to differentiate between Good Touch and Bad Touch — 82
- Tips for Teachers on how to teach their students about the POCSO Act — 85
- Tips and Exercises to Save the Environment — 87
- Tips for Teaching Children Respect for Diversity and Equality — 94
- Exercises to Promote Cleanliness in Kids — 97

Appendix — 101

Glossary — 105

Publisher's Note

In today's world, it is heartening to witness individuals standing up for their rights with passion and conviction. However, amidst this fervour, it becomes essential to pause and reflect on the responsibilities and duties that often seem to be overlooked. What are these responsibilities, and why do they not receive the same attention? This book seeks to address these questions by focusing on the fundamental duties enshrined in the Constitution of India, an aspect that is as vital as the rights we cherish.

Inspired by the visionary New Education Policy 2020, this book is designed to introduce to children, the concept of fundamental duties in an engaging and relatable manner. It emphasises the importance of striking a balance between individual rights and responsibilities, fostering a sense of accountability towards society, the environment, and the nation.

Told through a compelling story, the book integrates activities such as games and interdisciplinary exercises to make the learning experience interactive and enjoyable. These activities are crafted to encourage critical thinking, creativity, and a deeper understanding of how each individual can contribute to creating a more harmonious and equitable society.

The book aims to empower young readers with the knowledge and motivation to embrace their duties and grow up as responsible citizens. It is a call to action for children to not only recognise their rights but also to actively participate in building a society where every individual contributes to collective well-being.

We are proud to bring this important book to you and hope that it will play a significant role in shaping young minds and inspiring a brighter future for India!

Happy Reading!

PREAMBLE

WE, THE PEOPLE OF INDIA,
having solemnly resolved to constitute India into a
SOVEREIGN SOCIALIST
SECULAR DEMOCRATIC REPUBLIC
and to secure to all its citizens :
JUSTICE, social, economic and political;
LIBERTY of thought, expression,
belief, faith and worship;
EQUALITY of status and of opportunity;
and to promote among them all
FRATERNITY assuring the dignity of the
individual and the unity and
integrity of the Nation;
IN OUR CONSTITUENT ASSEMBLY
this twenty-sixth day of November, 1949, do
HEREBY ADOPT, ENACT AND GIVE TO
OURSELVES THIS CONSTITUTION.

A Trip to Kartavya Path

Forty excited students from class eight of a big Delhi school were all set for a fun trip to the Kartavya Path, near the famous India Gate. They gathered at school at 8 am, buzzing with energy. After a quick roll call and some strict dos and don'ts from their teacher, Sunita Ma'am, they hopped onto a bus and were off to Central Delhi!

The children reached the destination by 9.30 am and looked around in awe. On one side stood the grand Rashtrapati Bhavan, and on the other, the iconic India Gate—two of the most famous landmarks in the country!

Rashtrapati Bhavan, the official home of India's President, is a masterpiece, Sunita Ma'am told the children.

The first and last British Viceroys to live in Rashtrapati Bhavan were Lord Irwin and Edward Mountbatten. But in 1948, something amazing happened— the only Indian Governor General of India, C Rajagopalachari, moved in.

After India gained Independence in 1947, the Viceroy's House was renamed Rashtrapati Bhavan and became the official residence of the President of India.

Did you know?

It took 17 years to build Rashtrapati Bhavan. Construction started in 1912 and finished in 1929. It was designed by a brilliant British architect, Edwin Lutyens, with help from Herbert Baker. Back then, it was called Viceroy's House because British Viceroys lived there.

Rashtrapati Bhavan consists of 340 rooms in the main building and is built on a 130-hectare (320-acre area), officially called the Presidential Estate. The Estate also includes the presidential gardens, large open spaces, residences of bodyguards and staff, stables, other offices, including a battalion of the Indian Army. It also houses Amrit Udyan (formerly known as the Mughal Garden) which is situated at the back of the building, and is open to the public from February to March, every year.

On the other end of the road is the India Gate, a monument to the 74,187 soldiers of the Indian Army who were martyred in the first World War. After the Bangladesh Liberation War in 1972, a black marble plinth with a reversed rifle, capped by a war helmet and bounded by four eternal flames, was built beneath the archway. This structure, called the Amar Jawan Jyoti (Flame of the Immortal Soldier), has since 1971 served as India's tomb of the unknown soldier, and a salute to all those unknown martyrs who have laid their lives for the country.

On January 21, 2022, the flame was ceremoniously merged with the eternal flame at the National War Memorial, 400 metres away.

As they were sitting chatting on the grass and thinking about the history that this place has seen, one of the boys, Aman, spotted a small replica of the Indian flag, flying in the wind. All of a sudden, all eyes were on Aman and the flag.

Aman: Ma'am, look at this, we found this flag flying around on the grounds of the Kartavya Path!

Teacher: Oh, no. Who has left it here so carelessly? It is wrong to leave it around like this; it is an insult to our national flag! It is our duty to always respect it!

Aman: Duty? I don't understand, ma'am.

Teacher: As citizens of India, we are obligated to perform some duties towards our country and fellow men. These duties have been written in our Constitution.

Swati: Yes, we will be studying the Constitution this year. I have seen a chapter on 'The Constitution' in my textbook. What are these duties, ma'am?

Jatin: Yes! We want to know more about our duties and the Constitution, ma'am!

Teacher: Okay, so today, we all shall learn about the fundamental duties of every citizen of India! The 'Fundamental Duties' can be found in Part III of the Indian Constitution from Article 12 to 35. They can be applied to different aspects of India, such as our race, place of birth, religion, caste, creed, gender, and equality of opportunity in matters of employment.

Preeti: How many Fundamental Duties are there, ma'am?

Teacher: There are 10 principal Fundamental Duties listed in the Constitution. They were added to the constitution by the 42nd Amendment in 1976. An 11th duty was added in 2002.

Aman: How did people decide the number of Fundamental Duties? Did they borrow the idea of Fundamental Duties from the Constitution document of another country?

Teacher: You are right, Aman. The concept of the Fundamental Duties was taken from the USSR (Union of Soviet

Socialist Republic), now known as Russia. India's first Prime Minister, Jawaharlal Nehru, was very impressed by the endurance and might of the people of the USSR. He had witnessed the country transform from a feudal state to communism, effectively giving the power to its citizens and working class. For India, which had been plundered by the British for 200 years, it was very important that we first become self-sufficient. A constitution that ensures that all people are treated equally is a step forward in the direction of progress.

Preeti: Why are the Fundamental Duties so important, ma'am?

Teacher: They are important because they guide the people of India to be better citizens. By upholding our duties, we not only serve the country, but also our fellow people.

Aman: But ma'am, before telling us about each Fundamental Duty, can you tell us more about the Constitution? Why is it so important for the country?

Teacher: Yes, of course, Aman. Let's learn about the Constitution before we talk about our fundamental duties.

Constitution is a rulebook

Have you ever wondered how India is governed? Who makes the rules and why? Well, there is this very special rulebook called the Constitution of India that tells everyone how things should work in the country. From the Prime Minister to ordinary people like you and me, everyone has to follow it.

Just like you need rules when playing a game with friends to make sure everything is fair, India needs this Constitution to make sure the country runs smoothly and fairly for everyone.

Why did we need a Constitution?

India got its freedom from British rule in 1947. Imagine moving into a brand-new house with your family—you'd need some rules, right? Like who gets which room, how to share the spaces, and how to live together happily. Just like that, when India became free, our country needed a set of rules too. India was like a giant house with millions of people. We needed rules to make sure everyone could live together peacefully and happily.

India is special because it's like a big family. People speak different languages, follow different religions, and have different customs. Just like parents make rules that are fair for all their children, India needed fair rules for everyone.

Back then, some people were treated unfairly because of things like caste or whether they were rich or poor. The Constitution became a promise: 'Everyone is equal. Everyone matters.' It's just like when you make a rule in a game that no one can be left out, no matter how different they are. Isn't that a great way to make sure everyone feels included?

When was the Constitution adopted?

The Constitution of India was adopted on November 26, 1949, by the Constituent Assembly of India. But, it came into effect only on January 26, 1950, which is celebrated as the Republic Day in India. The Constituent Assembly was formed in 1946 to draft or write down the Constitution. Dr B R Ambedkar was the chairman of the Drafting Committee. The assembly took three years from December 1946 to November 1949 to draft it. The final document was signed by the 284 members of the Constituent Assembly. It is the longest written constitution of any sovereign country in the world, and the most important document of our nation. It contains all the rights that are bestowed upon us by the architects of India. It assures equal rights and opportunity to all the citizens and safeguards all of us from being taken advantage of by others.

There is no higher authority in India than the Constitution and we must all follow the preamble or introductory statements that set out its objectives of justice, liberty, equality and fraternity.

Fundamental Duty 1

Pride in Our National Flag

To oblige with the Indian Constitution and respect the National Anthem and Flag.

As she looked upon the Kartavya Path, the teacher recognised the importance of the national symbols that are needed to hold together a nation's identity. India's National Anthem, and its flag are two of the most prominent totems of our country that deserve to be respected at all times.

Teacher: We must always respect our National Anthem and flag. We should not take part in any activity that spoils the pride of our country. Our national flag is a symbol of the values that are inherent to our nation, and serve as a reminder of the sacrifices made by our freedom fighters in their pursuit of freedom from the British. It should always be allowed to fly tall, and never be lowered and disrespected. We should also be vigilant and stand upright whenever our National

Anthem plays. We should greet the lyrics written by Rabindranath Tagore with a sense of pride as the citizens of this great country.

Aman: There are a lot of people who don't get up when the National Anthem is played, ma'am. And if they do stand up, they keep jerking this way and that, which is insulting to our National Anthem.

Teacher: Yes, it is very irresponsible to act like this when the song is playing. We must always call out such people and tell them that their actions are shameful and undisciplined!

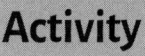 **National Symbol Explorer**

Step 1: Crack the Clues!

Read the riddles below and guess which national symbol they are talking about.

1. I have three colors and fly high in the sky, I stand for courage, peace, and growth, oh my! (What am I?)

2. I am sung with pride, standing tall, My words unite Indians, one and all! (What am I?)

3. I am a book, but not just any, I hold the laws for all, so fair and steady! (What am I?)

Step 2: Create Your Own National Symbol!

Imagine India is creating a new national symbol to celebrate the future! What would it be?

1. A New National Animal? What creature best represents the spirit of young India? Draw and describe it!

2. A Super Anthem Remix! If you could add one new line to the National Anthem, what would it say? Write it and explain why!

3. Your Own Mini Constitution! If you were writing three golden rules for a happy and fair school, what would they be? Write them like a mini Constitution!

Step 3: Share & Celebrate!

1. Present your new national symbol to your family or class. Vote on the most creative idea!
2. The winner gets the title of "Young Guardian of India" and a round of applause!

Write or draw

> **Fundamental Duty 2**

The Freedom Struggle

To cherish and follow the noble ideas that inspired the national struggle for freedom.

India's struggle for freedom against the British is one of the most poignant chapters in our history. It was based on the noble beliefs of freedom fighters who gave their lives so that our country could breathe without the noose of colonisation around its throat.

Teacher: India's fight for freedom is one of the most inspiring stories in history. Brave men and women gave their lives so we could live in an independent country. But do you think just reading about them in books is enough?

Jatin: We have read all about these brave men and women in our social science class, ma'am.

Teacher: Yes, you have, but that is not enough. We must learn from the brave acts and sacrifices of the freedom fighters, so that we can also honour their memories.

It isn't enough to just learn facts about Mahatma Gandhi and Bhagat Singh. We must also understand the ideas that guided them towards a path to fight for freedom!

Preeti: My great-grandfather was a freedom fighter who went to jail for his part in the Civil Disobedience Movement! My grandfather told me and my brother about his brave and courageous nature and how he defied the powerful British officers to shout the slogan of *Inquilab Zindabad* in front of them!

Teacher: Thank you for sharing that anecdote with us, Preeti. As you all can see, it isn't just the most famous freedom fighters whose stories are etched in our history books, but also about the ones who have been forgotten by historians. Their tales of bravery and courage are just as important. Their resilience, and undaunted spirit is what helped us gain freedom!

Aman: That means many of us might have freedom fighters in our own families too!

Teacher: Exactly! The spirit of bravery and resilience runs through generations. That's why we must remember and honour all those who fought for India's freedom—both the well-known leaders and the forgotten warriors who played a crucial role.

All the children nodded in unison. They felt a sudden surge of pride in their chests as they thought about all the brave men and women who had given up their lives, and made impossible sacrifices to free their country from the bondage of the British. They also realised how difficult it might have been to live under British rule years ago. They had heard about all the atrocities that the British committed against the Indian people for 200 years and were more astounded by the immense courage of the men and women who stood against the empire and helped to bring it to its knees.

Activity: Time Travel Mission

Mission Brief

You have been chosen as a Time Travel Explorer to visit India's past! Your goal? Meet a legendary freedom fighter and bring back their story to inspire the future!

Step 1: Choose Your Time Destination!

Pick a time in history—the Salt March (1930), the Quit India Movement (1942), or another major event.

Step 2: Interview a Freedom Fighter!

Imagine you get to talk to a freedom fighter in that time period. Write down:

- Their name and the year you met them.
- Three questions you would ask them about their fight for freedom.
- Their inspiring answers (use your imagination and research!).

Step 3: Create Your Time Travel Journal!

Draw or write about one freedom fighter you admire. You can:

- Draw a sketch of your meeting with the freedom fighter.
- Write a diary entry about what you saw, felt, and learned
- Design a 'Time Capsule' by drawing or listing symbols of freedom (spinning wheel, tricolor flag, etc.).

Step 4: Share Your Journey!

Tell your classmates, friends, or family about your adventure. Would you have joined the freedom movement? Why?

Write or draw

> **Fundamental Duty 3**

Public Property Belongs to all of Us

To safeguard all public property.

One of the many responsibilities of a teachers is to educate their students about etiquette. They should teach the students to always be responsible in public and never take part in any activity that spoils other's properties and historical monuments. This also inculcates a habit of cleanliness and discipline among the kids.

Teacher: Have you ever seen someone scribbling on a wall or breaking a park bench? How did you feel when you saw that?

Aman: Yes, ma'am! Last week, I saw someone drawing on the walls of our school bathroom. It looked so bad!

Swati: When I went to see Red Fort, a group of men used a small, blunt object and tried to scratch their names on its walls before they were stopped by the security guards!

Teacher: It is very bad to deface the walls of centuries-old monuments that have been hailed for their architectural beauty and for their place in our history. We must always remain vigilant, and never allow people to spoil public property by scratching their names on it or painting graffiti on the walls. You can see all kinds of strange things written on the outer walls of famous buildings, including the walls of the underpasses in the city.

Jatin: But what can we do to stop these horrible people, ma'am? They won't listen to children!

Teacher: We must always alert the authorities when we see any person spoiling public property.

Aman: What about people who spit on the roads, and throw garbage and plastic around without any regard for public hygiene? They even deface walls and don't even try to find the nearest *Sulabh Shauchalaya* or a public restroom!

Teacher: The best way to combat littering and public spitting and treating the whole world as their personal bathroom is to spread awareness that it is wrong to do such activities outdoors. Besides, they are polluting the environment and spoiling the area for everyone. They must learn or be reported to the authorities.

Jatin: But people never listen if you tell them not to litter or spit on the roads! Instead, they get angry and start fighting with the person who dares to tell them not to dirty the place.

Teacher: I understand that people get defensive when they are called out on their mistakes and this can often lead to such abrasive behaviour. The best thing to do in such a situation is to ask the person politely if they would like to pick up the trash they have thrown and put it in a dustbin instead. But, if they get angry, then don't talk with them because they won't understand your pleas and you should keep away from such anti-social people. Remember children, your safety comes first.

Swati: But that way, people will never learn to take responsibility for their own actions. We can't expect the sweepers to do all the work as if they are our slaves. Shouldn't we work together to make our cities, towns and villages cleaner and more hygienic?

Teacher: You're absolutely right, Swati. And the process to become more responsible has to start with government campaigns that encourage people to be more aware of their surroundings. They should be taught that littering is wrong and that it is always better to seek a public dustbin than spit or throw

garbage on the road. Additionally, the government should also place security directives at every heritage site to prevent people from defacing the property.

"Duty is not a matter of obligation, but a path of honor. In serving our nation, we serve ourselves."

- Anonymous

Activity: Guardians of Public Spaces

Step 1: Spy on Your Surroundings!

Look around your neighborhood, school, or any public space. Find these places:

- Parks & Playgrounds – Do they look clean and safe?
- Libraries & Schools – Are the books and walls neat?
- Bus Stops & Train Stations – Are they tidy, or do you see litter?

Secret Task:

- Sketch or describe a public place near you.
- Write down anything that needs fixing or protection.

Mission Briefing:

- Hello, young heroes! You have been chosen for a top-secret mission: To protect and care for public spaces!
- Your task is to observe, report, and take action to keep our shared places safe and beautiful. Are you ready? Let's go!

Step 2: The Hero's Code!

All great heroes follow a code of honor. Create your own pledge to protect public property!

Complete this:

- I, (your name), promise to protect public spaces by _____.
- If I see someone harming public property, I will _____.
- One small action I can take today to make my surroundings better is _____.

Make it official! Sign your pledge and hang it up where you can see it!

Step 3: The Action Challenge!

- Act it out! Pretend to be a superhero saving a park from litter or stopping someone from damaging a monument.
- Capture the moment! Take a picture of a clean public space and share why it's important.
- Spread the word! Teach your friends and family the importance of caring for public places.

Write or draw

> **Fundamental Duty 4**

Preserve the Unity of Our Nation

To protect the integrity, sovereignty, and unity of India.

An essential feature of being a good citizen is respecting the values and beliefs of everyone.

Teacher: United we stand, divided we fall! We should always resist other people's attempts to divide us. If we stand united in front of our enemies, they will be unable to defeat us!

Aman: But who are our enemies, ma'am?

Teacher: Our enemies are people who seek to divide us on the basis of class, caste and religion. They sow the seeds of hatred and animosity between communities and reap the benefits of the division they've caused. If we stop fighting with each other over petty issues, and instead work on building the nation together, we will become even more prosperous and powerful.

Swati: How can we achieve such a task, ma'am?

Teacher: When we interact with people from different communities, we get to know more about them. This helps us to get rid of our biases and prejudices against them. We must always work to know other people better, so that we can form better connections with them. The only way to build communal harmony is by breaking down the barriers that we have built around us. We must understand that all human beings seek the same things—a good life with their families, education, peace, and happiness—even though we may pray to different gods.

Jatin: Umm, we could start by personally meeting people. Maybe, we could hold an event in which people from different communities could participate and talk about their culture.

Teacher: That's a brilliant idea, Jatin! We can do that even in school. We can have people of different faiths talk to the other children in the class about the customs and festivals they follow, so that we all understand each other better.

Preeti: But what if the children start to argue there like some adults and a fight breaks out?

Teacher: A very good question, indeed! Does anyone have a solution to this problem?

Aman: We can put up charts around the classroom that we must be polite to each other and if adults have such meetings, they can have boards put up at the entrance to the hall that only civil discourse is allowed at such meetings. Or better yet, why don't we start by producing TV shows where such interfaith unity between people of different religions can be talked about without fear of violence. We could also hold radio shows that'd be able to reach different regions in India where people do not have television or the internet.

Teacher: This will ensure that the correct information reaches everyone and will also reduce the threat of inter-community violence.

Activity — Unity is Powerful

An essential feature of being a good citizen is respecting the values and beliefs of everyone.

The Unity Puzzle
Let's build a puzzle together!
Your teacher will give you a puzzle piece.

On it, write one thing that makes India special. Some ideas:

- Our different languages.
- Our colourful festivals.
- Our delicious foods.
- Our different traditions and customs.
- Our love for one another.

Now, put all the pieces together to form a big "Unity Puzzle." This shows that even though we are all different, together, we make India strong!

Write or draw

Fundamental Duty 5

Our National Heritage

To cherish and preserve the rich national heritage of our composite culture.

A country as diverse as India draws strength from its many cultures and religions. The teacher was very excited to teach the students about how they should never be ashamed of their cultures, but celebrate what is unique about them.

Teacher: India has a colourful and varied culture! We are different from each other, but our differences don't divide us. Instead, they highlight the rich variety and diversity that our land possesses! We must preserve the rich heritage that has been passed down to us by our ancestors and broaden our knowledge of different cultures that thrive in India so wonderfully, together.

Jatin: How can we do that, ma'am?

Teacher: By getting closer to our roots, and identifying our own unique cultural prints, we can assure that they are preserved and cherished. We need to respect the rich history of our country, and respect all the different cultures that it has birthed. If we stay in contact with the people around us, and display general inquisitiveness, we will be able to keep our cultural practices intact.

Preeti: We should also listen to our elders and remember their life stories. That way, we might be able to better understand our history on a more personal level. By making sure that we know where we come from, and respecting our roots, we might be able to preserve our past history and save it from being forgotten.

Teacher: Yes, we must listen to what our elders say because their stories harbour the history of India and its cultural practices.

Activity: Guardians of Our National Heritage!

1. The Creativity Zone

Write or Draw:

- A monument you'd love to visit!
- A dance move from an Indian dance form.
- A festival memory you cherish!
- A food dish your family loves to cook!

2. The Challenge Riddles

Can you name?

Solve these riddles to unlock the secrets of India's culture!

Monument Mystery

- "I stand tall with white marble walls,
  A symbol of love, admired by all! What am I?"
  (Answer: Taj Mahal)

Dancing Feet Challenge

- "With graceful moves and bells that chime,
  This classical dance has stood the test of time!"
  (Answer: Bharatanatyam/Kathak/Odissi)

Festive Sparkles

- "I bring colors, light, and sweets,
  With joy and love, everyone meets!"
  (Answer: Diwali/Holi)

Tasty Traditions

- "I'm spicy, sweet, or filled with ghee,
  Your state is known for dishes like me!"

Write or draw

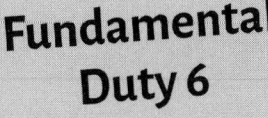

Develop a Spirit of Inquiry

To develop scientific temper, humanism, and spirit of inquiry.

The children were taught science in their school, and some were even good at the subject. However, their teacher wanted them to always have an open mind. Reading books, and learning facts was a very nice way of getting good marks in tests.

Teacher: Have you ever wondered how airplanes fly, why the sky changes colors, or how your favorite gadgets work? Science is all around us, and the more we question, the more we discover!

Aman: Yes, ma'am! Airplanes fly because of the force of lift created by their wings. The sky changes colors due to the scattering of light, and gadgets work using different scientific principles like electricity and magnetism!

Teacher: To ask questions, and seek wisdom is the only way towards enlightenment! You all should keep a

scientific temperament and be curious about your surroundings! That way, you can learn new things everyday that'll help you grow smart!

Swati: Our school's science fair gives us a very good opportunity to experiment and have fun with science. It also helps us learn new things and rare facts!

Aman: We should always focus on the practical uses of science and perform activities that help us understand basic concepts easily.

Teacher: Science goes hand in hand with the need to connect with our fellow human beings. Apart from learning about technology and making scientific discoveries, we should also make space for each other. To understand a fellow human being's emotions, and learning to empathise with their sufferings will keep the spirit of humanism alive in each one of us.

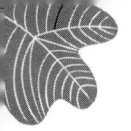

Activity: Be a Curious Explorer!

Develop a Spirit of Inquiry

To develop scientific temper, humanism, and spirit of inquiry

Objective: Encourage students to develop a questioning mindset and explore the world around them.

How to Play

- Look Around! Ask students to observe their surroundings—classroom, playground, nature, or even objects in their bag.
- Ask a Question! Each student must come up with one "Why," "How," or "What" question about something they see. (Example: Why do leaves change color? or How does a fan work?)
- Pass the Question! Students take turns asking their question to a classmate, who must either try to answer it or pass it to another friend for help.
- Find the Answer! If no one knows the answer, they can look it up in a book, ask a teacher, or do a simple experiment at home to discover the truth!

Write or draw

> **Fundamental Duty 7**

Right to Education

To provide opportunities for education to children between 6-14 years of age, and duty as parents to ensure that such opportunities are being awarded to their child.

The teacher looked around the class, at every child who was lucky to be receiving education from one of the best schools in Delhi. At the same time, she felt sad for all the children who are unable to go to school for many reasons. She wanted to educate her students about this problem, and how the constitution has tried to solve it.

Teacher: Imagine a world where some children go to school, learn, and chase their dreams, while others never get the chance to read or write. How would that make you feel?

Preeti: That would be so unfair! Every child should have the right to learn.

Teacher: Exactly! Education is a fundamental right under our Constitution, and it is our responsibility to ensure that no child is left behind.

Preeti: It is very sad that a lot of students don't get education because of the financial condition of their family. What should be done in such a sad situation?

Teacher: But what do you think are some of the reasons why many children in India still don't get an education?

Aman: Some children have to work to support their families instead of going to school.

Swati: Yes! And in some villages, schools are too far away, or there aren't enough teachers.

Teacher: That's true. Many challenges prevent children from getting an education, but our Constitution guarantees the Right to Education (Article 21A) for all children aged 6 to 14 years. This means every child in India has the legal right to go to school for free!

Swati: That's great! But if it's a law, then why do so many children still miss out on school?

Teacher: That's because laws need people like us to make sure they are followed. We can all do something to help. Can you think of ways we can support education for all?

Preeti: We can donate books and stationery to children who can't afford them!

Aman: We can help teach younger kids who don't have access to tuition.

Swati: We can raise awareness about the importance of education in our communities!

Teacher: Wonderful ideas! Now, let's do a fun activity to understand how education builds a strong nation.

Note

The Right to Education (RTE) Act, 2009 ensures that every child in India between the ages of 6 to 14 years has the right to free and compulsory education in a neighbourhood school. It also mandates that private schools reserve 25% of their seats for children from economically weaker sections. The act helps bridge the gap between privileged and underprivileged children, ensuring that no child is denied education due to financial difficulties.

Activity: Education is My Superpower!

1. **The Treasure Hunt of Learning!**
   - Imagine education is a treasure chest filled with magical powers! What do you think learning gives you?

2. **The "magic power" of some things you do everyday:**

   - Reading books → Takes you to magical places
   - Writing stories → Lets you share your imagination
   - Solving math problems → Helps build houses, bridges, and rockets!
   - Learning about nature → Teaches you how to protect the Earth
   - Drawing and music → Helps express feelings in fun ways!

3. **Draw a treasure chest and write or draw what you love learning**

The School of Dreams

Imagine you are opening a school.
Think about:

- What would you name your school?
- What subjects would you teach?
- How would you make learning fun for all children?

Write or draw

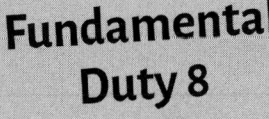

This Earth Belongs to all of Us

To protect and improve the natural environment including lakes, wildlife, rivers, and forests.

As years have progressed, the threat of global warming has become an alarming reality. The constant change in the weather, and the increase in the temperature during summer is very alarming. To combat this emergency, it is important that every child is taught to treat nature with love and try to preserve all its riches.

Teacher: Look around you! Nature has given us so much—clean air, water, and beautiful landscapes. But have you noticed how the summers are getting hotter and the weather is becoming unpredictable? That's because of climate change, and it's a serious problem we must all work to solve.

Aman: I get very scared by the condition of our planet. The way climate change is affecting us is very scary!

Swati: It has become unbearably hot in the summers, and winters are getting colder. During the monsoons, it rains so much that entire roads are flooded. Of late, in some cities, you get so much rain on one day alone, whereas in earlier years, that amount of rain would fall over the entire monsoon season! It becomes very dangerous for people to go from one place to another! In the hills there are landslides and even roads get washed away.

In the summer, forest fires can cause havoc. Look at what happened in Los Angeles in America recently. Industries are dumping chemicals and plastic into the sea.

Teacher: Your concerns about the growing severity of climate change are absolutely valid, children. It is indeed scary to see how quickly the environment is deteriorating. However, our concerns are futile unless we do something to change the situation. How many of you have heard about Greta Thunberg?

Preeti: She is a climate activist who went on a school strike to speak on climate change and attempted to persuade the Swiss Government to adhere to the 2015 Paris Climate Agreement.

Teacher: Yes, Greta Thunberg is a very brave young woman who is an example of how climate activism can

make an impact on the masses. Her resilience and determination to build a better future for our children is awe inspiring. Like her, we all must speak up about climate change. We must not only help in growing trees around us, but also raise our voices against industries that dump chemical waste in the sea, or have acres of valuable forest land being cleared for the industry and governments to build more concrete cities. There is no point in trying to build more cities if none of us ever get to live in them!

Instead, our priority should be to protect our natural resources and cease any activities that harm our environment.

Jatin: We can't let our fellow human beings, flora and fauna suffer the effects of worsening climate. I will not only plant trees at all favourable spots that I see around my house, but also spread more information about how best we can treat our environment.

Preeti: I will write a letter to our school principal and request her to organise a talk or seminar in school so that we can all learn the ways to ease Climate Change. This way, every student will get an understanding of how best to act in order to save our precious earth.

Activity: You are a Guardian of the Earth!

Students will take on the role of detectives to uncover environmental problems, discuss their impact, and propose creative solutions in a fun, interactive way!

How to Play

Set the Scene

Story

A villain named Dr Waste is harming our planet! He pollutes rivers, cuts down trees, and fills the air with smoke. Our mission is to find his clues, solve the mystery, and save Earth!

Clue Hunt

Six mystery envelopes are hidden around the classroom. Each contains a riddle or picture about an environmental issue (e.g., plastic pollution, deforestation, air pollution).

Clue 1

I am everywhere, but I take 500 years to disappear. I harm sea animals and birds. What am I?

Clue 2

I help you breathe, but people cut me down for paper and land. What am I?

Answer: Trees! Deforestation!

Solution: Plant more trees, use less paper, support reforestation projects.

Clue 3

You cannot see me, but when I get dirty, people cough and fall sick. What am I?

Answer: Air pollution!
Solution: Use bicycles, avoid burning garbage, plant trees.

Detectives at Work

Students form small Eco-Detective Teams and search for the hidden clues. After finding one, they read it aloud, discuss the problem, and brainstorm two solutions to fix it.

Mission Report

Each team presents their findings and acts out a creative way to solve the issue.

Write or draw

> **Fundamental Duty 9**

Let Our Country be a Centre of Excellence

To strive towards excellence in all genres of individual and collective activities.

The teacher knew that her students had a lot of different aspirations that extended far beyond academics. She hoped that they'd all excel in their fields, and draw inspiration from their idols.

Teacher: Imagine it's 10 years from now—what are you doing? Are you designing skyscrapers, saving lives, writing books, or exploring space? Tell me, children, what do you want to become when you grow up?

Jatin: My parents want me to excel in studies, but I want to be a cricketer!

Aman: I want to be a dancer!

Swati: I want to be an astronaut!

Preeti: I want to be a writer!

Teacher: See, how diverse your dreams are! It is important that we seek excellence in a variety to activities in our life. We should all try at least one sport, learn to dance and sing, or draw or swim just so we can take advantage of all the gifts that have been bestowed upon us. How will we know that we are good at something unless and until we try it? Never shy away from trying new things and working towards perfection!

Jatin: Ma'am, our schools should help us in finding our true potential. If we are exposed to sports, academic, and cultural activities and are free to try everything, not only will we be able to discover our future vocation, but we will also learn many interesting things.

Teacher: Yes, it is the school's responsibility to provide the best facilities to its students so that they get a taste of every possible opportunity and things that excite them.

Activity: My Path to Excellence

Objective: Encourage children to think about how they can contribute to excellence in their country through their own actions.

The Great Talent Hunt!

Teacher's Question: What makes YOU special?

Activity: Give students 2 minutes to think of one thing they're amazing at (singing, solving puzzles, helping friends, playing sports, storytelling, etc.).

Fun Twist: Each student shares their talent in a single dramatic or funny sentence—I am the superhero of sketching! or I can solve math puzzles faster than a ninja!

The Role-Play Challenge!

Activity: Students pair up and pick a real-life situation where they can make a difference (e.g., stopping littering, helping a classmate, being kind to animals).

Action: They create and perform a short skit or act out how they would handle the situation.

Exciting Twist: The class votes for the most inspiring, funniest, and most creative performances!

Write or draw

> **Fundamental Duty 10**

Everyone is Equal, Respect One-another

To promote the spirit of harmony and brotherhood amongst all the people of India and renounce any practices that are derogatory to women.

Women's safety has become one of the most debated topics in India today. The teacher was very concerned for the girls in her class and beyond. She wanted each and every one of them to know that they were safe and loved. It was also important to tell the boys that respecting women was one of their chief duties as the citizens of India.

Teacher: Can you think of a woman—whether in your family, school, or history—who has inspired you? What makes her special?

Aisha: My mother inspires me because she works hard at her job and takes care of our family. She never gives up, no matter how tough things get!

Teacher: That's wonderful! Women have contributed to society

in every field—science, sports, politics, arts, and more. But despite these achievements, many women still face discrimination.

Swati: There are so many girls who don't feel safe outside because they are afraid that men will harm them. My cousin sister told me that she was catcalled while she was returning home from her college just a few days ago!

Preeti: Respecting women and building an environment where everyone feels equal is important if we want to progress as a nation. No matter what, we should never use derogatory language and behaviour against women.

I remember a group of boys kept staring at me while I was with my mother at the market! I just don't understand why this happens and what must be done to make all women safe inside and outside their homes!

Teacher: I'm really sorry that you had to go through a terrible experience like that, Preeti. A lot of women, including my friends have been catcalled, stared at or groped in public. Even I have even been subjected to vulgar leering in the Metro and on public buses! However, I'd

	like to ask the boys about their opinion on women's safety and how they are going to ensure that we women never feel unsafe with them.
Aman:	I think it is important for boys to learn in childhood that girls should be seen with respect. They are not inferior to us, but are our equals.
Teacher:	If a boy sees his own parents discriminate between him and his sister at home, then he will grow up thinking that women shouldn't be given equal importance.
Jatin:	We must eradicate gender-based discrimination at home to ensure that this doesn't happen!
Teacher:	Yes, and we must teach boys that it doesn't matter if they are outside or inside the house, that every girl deserves respect because they are human beings and not objects.
Aman:	We should always call out men who catcall women, or display any kind of objectionable behaviour towards them.
Swati:	Schools should also hold seminars and classes for everyone so that they can understand that violence against women is a crime and should never happen.

Teacher: Exactly, it is up to adults to ascertain that children are brought up in the best possible way so that they learn to respect everyone—men and women, boys and girls, rich or poor, townspeople or country folk, from the very beginning. By instilling sensitivity and kindness in childhood, parents can avoid seeing their sons becoming men who are unkind to women.

Activity: We are all Special!

The Magic Mirror

- Imagine you have a magic mirror. When you look into it, you don't just see your face—you see what makes you special!

Now, think:

- What are three good things about yourself? (eg, "I am kind," "I am a good listener," "I love helping others.")
- What are three good things about a friend or classmate? (eg, "They share their toys," "They make me laugh," "They are helpful.")

The Respect Puzzle

- Let's build a puzzle together!

Your teacher will give you a puzzle piece. On it, write one way you can show respect to others. Some ideas:

- Speak politely to everyone.
- Share and take turns.
- Listen when someone is talking.
- Help a friend in need.

Once everyone has written their ideas, put the puzzle pieces together to make a "Respect Wall"!

Write or draw

> **Fundamental Duty 11**

Safeguard Our Nation

To defend the country and perform national services if and when the country requires.

The teacher told the children that all should learn an important fact—that one must always be loyal to one's own. She wanted them to feel patriotic towards India, and be ready to serve it whenever they are needed, in any capacity possible.

Teacher: India is our motherland and any threat against it should be answered with force. We must be ready to serve it whenever it needs us even if our contribution is limited.

Jatin: But we are children, ma'am, how can we defend our country against bigger threats?

Teacher: Nobody expects you to join the army at a young age, dear. What we must keep in mind is that it is our responsibility to always think about our country and do our best to protect its honour.

Preeti: We must never back down from confronting people who try to denigrate the name of our great nation!

Swati: Ma'am, is it possible to serve India without actually, physically fighting in the army?

Teacher: Yes! It important to understand that serving one's country doesn't mean that you have to become a soldier. By standing with your fellow citizens and protecting their rights, you can make a very big difference.

Aman: How important is it to be patriotic, ma'am?

Teacher: By being patriotic, and having a sense of pride in one's homeland is important because it is tied to our identity as Indians. If we don't feel good about our own home, then how will others perceive us?

Preeti: But does that mean we should be blind to the faults of the people around us, even when they are wrong? What about our leaders? Should we follow what they say without questioning them?

Teacher: Never! You must never stop questioning your leaders! There is a difference between patriotism and jingoism. Jingoism makes us want to look away from the flaws that affect the systems of our country and keep it from progressing. If we let our leaders get away with making bad decisions that harm the public, then we are also taking part in sowing the seeds of ruin for our country! It is best to examine a concept or idea from all angles before deciding whether it is good or bad for us. We must never look at our leaders as if they are our gods. They are in this position of power because of us, because we have elected them into that post and, thus they are meant to serve the country, first and foremost!

Jatin: What happens when someone fails to do these duties, ma'am?

Teacher: The constitution recommends us to follow our duties, but a lot of them must arise from our own personal learnings and experience. Our parents and teachers are responsible for fostering these values in us while we are still young so that we are able to fully absorb them and enact them in our daily lives.

Preeti: What if we forget these duties, ma'am? Will we be punished for it?

Teacher: No, you won't be punished, Preeti, but isn't it better to practise these duties in our daily routine? If we do that, then effortlessly, we can make them a part of our lives.

Aman: From now on, I will try to practise all my duties and help others in following them as well.

All children in unison: YES! ME TOO!

Teacher: Wonderful! I'm glad that we took this trip and we all together had such a meaningful discussion! I believe that you all will fulfil your promises and pave a path of enlightenment for others as well.

All children: Thank you, ma'am!!

The children had had a long, yet eventful day, filled with a wealth of knowledge that left them both exhilarated and anxious. As they walked towards their bus, their footsteps slow and deliberate, each child's mind was abuzz with the day's learnings. The weight of newfound understanding settled upon their young shoulders, and they feared that the precious information might slip away once they returned to the familiar comfort of their homes.

Boarding the school bus, the children's thoughts drifted back to the important facts and profound lessons they had absorbed through the day. A sense of pride washed over them as they contemplated the privilege of being citizens of India. Yet, with this realisation came an acute awareness of the responsibilities that accompanied such an honour. They understood that to truly embody the values and beliefs envisioned by the great leaders who had penned the Constitution, they must diligently perform their duties as citizens.

As the bus pulled away from the India Gate area, a collective epiphany swept through the minds of the young passengers. The children lost in their own thoughts, came to the same conclusion—that this experience was etched in their memories. The significance of the day's lessons, the weight of their newfound responsibilities, and the pride in their heritage had turned into a transformative experience that would shape their perspectives for years to come.

Activity: The Nation's Helper Detective

Unscramble These Important Words!

Can you figure out who these real-life heroes are?

- RDIOSLES → _ _ _ _ _
- EPCOLI → _ _ _ _ _ _
- IEFRIGTFHRE → _ _ _ _ _ _ _ _ _ _ _
- TDOCRO → _ _ _ _ _ _
- RUSEN → _ _ _ _ _
- CITOMMNUY HERO → _ _ _ _ _ _ _ _ _ _ _ _ _

Name the hero

- Protects the country from threats
- Maintains law and order
- Saves people from fires
- Treats sick and injured people
- Cares for patients in hospitals
- Helps the community in emergencies

Write or draw

Beyond Fundamental Duties

1. The POCSO Act of 2012

After coming back from the picnic, all the children felt refreshed and enlightened. They had a renewed faith in their ability to serve their nation as well. Everyone showed that they didn't forget their pledge to become better citizens of their country, and began to put efforts to make it a better place for everyone. They became cautious about public littering and always picked up their trash, while also encouraging other people to do their part in keeping the roads and premises of their country clean and healthy.

However, a tragedy struck the school a few days later. One of the students in sixth standard had gotten hurt. The children didn't know the details, because the school authorities didn't share them, but they knew that something truly bad had happened. Then, one day, they heard a term that they did not completely understand. The adult, who had hurt the child, would be tried under the 'POCSO Act' in the court. They had no idea what this meant, and decided to ask their teacher about it.

Aman: What is POCSO Act, ma'am?

At first, their teacher was surprised that the children had heard about the POCSO Act. Of course, the recent events had been terrible, and the school authorities had been very careful in avoiding any mention of the criminal act that had been committed against the child. But then, she realised that it was very important to let them know about this policy that has been enacted by the government of India to protect children against harm. And because this was a very sensitive topic, she had to explain her points clearly and carefully so that the children wouldn't get scared and panic.

Teacher: POCSO Act, which is short for Protection of Children Against Sexual Offences, is a law designed to protect children (under 18 years) from sexual abuse, harassment, and exploitation. It was passed by the Parliament of India on 22 May 2012.

The children were confused. They did not understand the meaning of sexual assault because their school did not teach Sexual education. They had never been told that there were people who could hurt them by crossing boundaries physically. The teacher knew this and she realised that she had to be very careful and not scare the kids.

Teacher: Okay, I'm going to teach you all about Good-touch and Bad-touch today.

The children leaned closer in their seats, focusing on what the teacher was saying. They knew that this was a very important topic, and they had to pay attention if they wanted to really understand it.

Teacher: There are two types of touch; Good Touch and Bad Touch. Good Touch is any physical contact that makes you feel safe, comfortable and pleasant. For example, when your parents hug you, or when you give a hi-five to your friend, or when you hold hands while crossing the road. Good Touch always assures you that you are not in danger. You don't feel strange, or scared.

The children remembered all the instances when they had felt comforted and safe while their parents hugged them or held their hands. They also had pleasant memories of playing with each other, and being rough-housed by one another, which is a common and universal experience of being a child.

Teacher: Bad Touch, however, is completely opposite of Good Touch. It is any physical contact that makes you feel uncomfortable, scared, or hurt. A slap by a parent or teacher for a mistake pay attention causes you pain. If someone tries to touch you on your private body parts, and tries to cross your physical boundaries with you, then they are engaging in the harmful Bad Touch.

Everyone was shocked to hear this. The children had experienced thrashing by their elders, and now understood that parents should have dealt with their naughty behaviour with other correctional methods such as being firm and not allowing the children to wilfully be naughty again. They could also think of instances when people like their own family friends, or older people, had touched them in a way that made them uncomfortable.

Teacher: It is very important to understand how to differentiate between Good Touch and Bad Touch. Your comfort should be your highest priority and this includes your relatives as well. A significant number of child sexual abuse cases in India involve the culprit who is a member of, or close to the victim's family.

This was a very surprising revelation for the children. Nobody had ever told them that their own family members could hurt them. They didn't know how to react to the fact that so many children just like them had been abused by their own relatives, the people whom they were supposed to trust and love.

Aman: But ma'am what should we do if we are uncomfortable after someone touches us?

Teacher: You should immediately tell your parents and/or guardian. It is extremely important that you tell a responsible adult about your experience because it can help catch the person and then hold them accountable for their actions. A lot of times, such people try to threaten the children by saying that if they tell anyone about what happened to them, they will do something horrible to their parents or physically harm them as well. This is why a lot of children don't come forward with their stories of abuse. While it is definitely very scary to tell someone that you experienced something very bad, children should never keep such things to themselves because it might lead to even more repeated abuse by the person.

Preeti: What if we tell our parents, and they don't believe us, ma'am?

The teacher knew that this question would come up. Children were, after all, too young to understand a lot of things and because of their inexperience, they are often not taken seriously by adults. This is very unfortunate because if parents or the guardian doesn't believe the child, it can lead to severe consequences. A lot of children lose faith in adults after their stories are not believed and then decide to never confess anything to anyone because they fear getting rejected.

Teacher: Every parent should take their child's report of such incidents very seriously. If they do not, then they are not doing their job as the protectors of their wards or minor children properly. If their child is talking about someone who is a close family member, then don't ignore or avoid the issue. Go all out and take action against the offender. Do not be afraid about what the society will say and think about their child or the culprit. Their first, and only responsibility is towards the welfare of their child.

Swati: How is all this related to the POCSO Act, ma'am?

Teacher: POCSO Act is a special law that was made in 2012 and works like a protective shield for all children, both boys and girls. It's here to keep you safe from three main types of wrong behaviours: sexual assault (when someone touches you inappropriately), sexual harassment (when someone makes you feel uncomfortable with their words or actions), and pornography (when someone shows you inappropriate pictures or videos or takes such pictures or videos of you).

There are special courts just for handling these cases, so you don't have to wait for a long time to get help. This means your case will be looked at quickly and carefully by people who understand how to talk to children.

The best part about this law is that it makes everything easier for children who need help. When you tell someone what happened, the police officers will be extra nice and gentle while talking to you. You'll meet special people who really understand children and know how to help them. The law makes sure that when you're telling your story, it's recorded in a way that doesn't make you repeat it many times, which could be upsetting. There are special judges who will listen to your story quickly and make sure you're protected. Everything you tell them will be kept private, just like a secret that keeps you safe.

The POCSO Act is a law that helps keep children safe from bad touch and unsafe behaviour. It makes sure that if someone does something wrong to a child, they can be punished.

This law protects children from:

1. Unsafe Touch—If someone touches a child in a way that makes them uncomfortable or asks them to touch someone else in a bad way, it's not okay.

2. Using Words or Actions in a Wrong Way—If someone says bad things, makes rude gestures, follows a child in a way

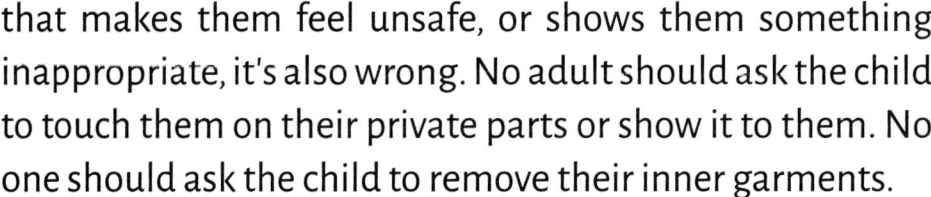

that makes them feel unsafe, or shows them something inappropriate, it's also wrong. No adult should ask the child to touch them on their private parts or show it to them. No one should ask the child to remove their inner garments.

3. Serious Harm—If someone tries to hurt a child's body in a very serious way, this law makes sure they are stopped and punished.

4. Show them or make dirty videos—or ask them to pose for dirty videos.

The teacher also told them that if anything like this ever happens, they should tell a trusted adult immediately—like a parent, teacher, or another grown-up they trust—so they can get help and stay safe.

There was a moment of silence in class as their teacher listed out all the ways in which somebody could cause them harm.

Teacher: I know that what I have told you now is very horrible but it is necessary that we hold such discussions with children in our classrooms. By introducing the concept of Good Touch and Bad Touch, and teaching children about how to detect signs of any harmful contact is very important. The POCSO act ensures that children who have been abused, will get quick justice and the culprit will be caught and tried without any delay. As always, it's never a child's fault if an adult touches them inappropriately and we must work together to smash the culture of shame so that the survivors of abuse can live their lives with their head held high.

How to differentiate between Good Touch and Bad Touch

Safe Touch Rules, Safe Touches Feel:

Comforting and caring
Like a gentle pat on the back
Like a welcome hug from family
Safe and makes you happy

Unsafe Touch Rules, Unsafe Touches Feel:

Uncomfortable or scary
Like they should be a secret
Confusing or wrong
Make you feel unsafe

Safe Touch Examples:

High-fives with friends
Doctor check-ups with parent present
Help with washing from trusted caregiver
Goodnight hugs from family

What To Do:

Say "NO" loudly
Get away quickly if possible
Tell a trusted adult right away
Never keep unsafe touches secret

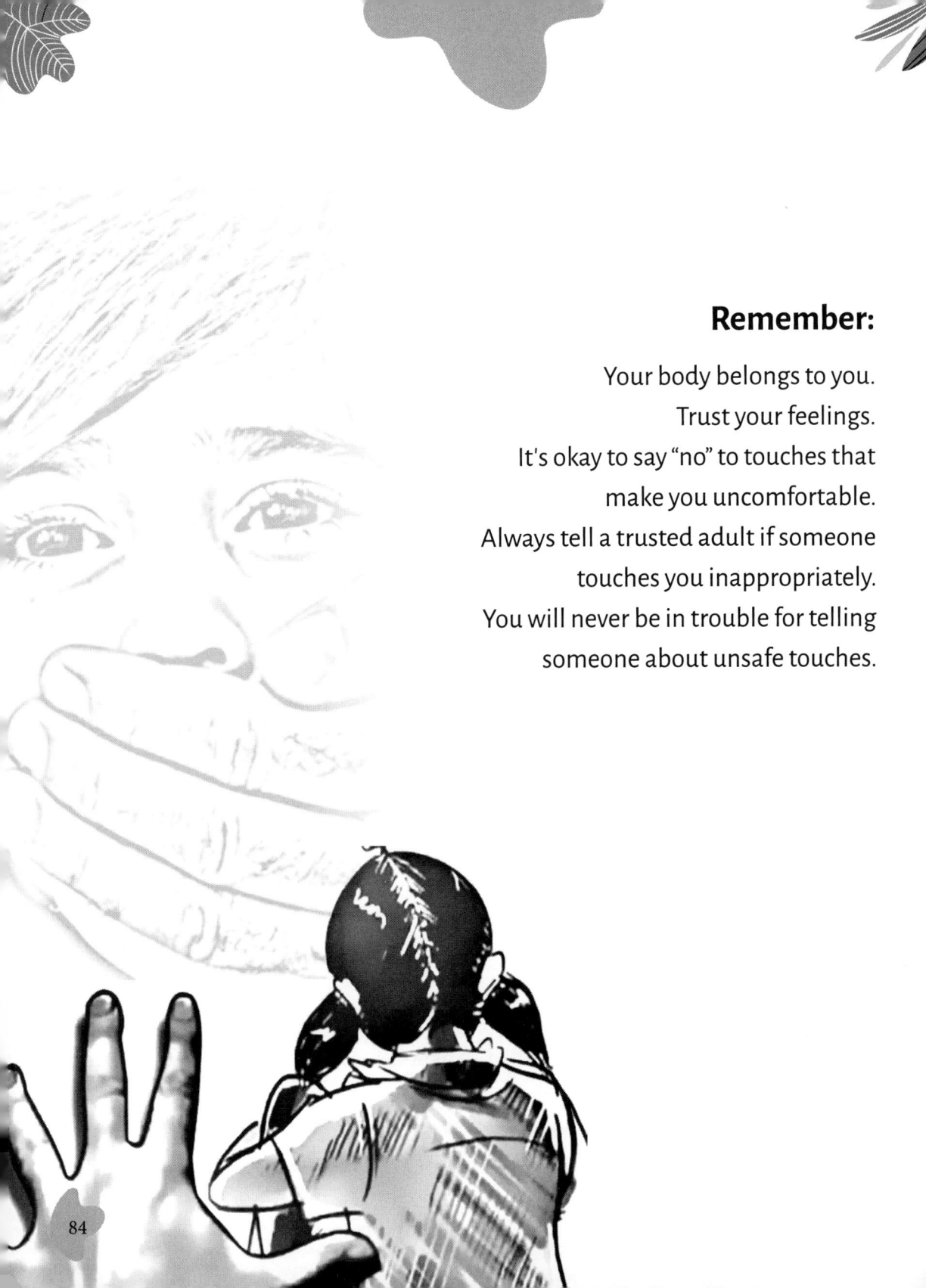

Remember:

Your body belongs to you.
Trust your feelings.
It's okay to say "no" to touches that make you uncomfortable.
Always tell a trusted adult if someone touches you inappropriately.
You will never be in trouble for telling someone about unsafe touches.

Tips for Teachers on how to teach their students about the POCSO Act

POCSO Act Key Points, Teaching About POCSO:

- Explain that there are laws to protect children
- Emphasise that help is always available
- Discuss the role of safe adults
- Explain confidential reporting
- Share emergency helpline numbers

Teacher's Responsibilities:

- Mandatory reporting of suspected abuse
- Maintaining confidentiality
- Supporting affected children
- Documenting concerns
- Coordinating with authorities

Response Protocol:
If a Child Talks About This:

- Stay calm and listen without judgement
- Believe the child and offer support
- Don't promise to keep secrets
- Document the disclosure immediately
- Follow the school's reporting procedure
- Maintain the child's privacy

Support Resources:

- Keep emergency contact numbers handy
- Know local child protection authorities
- Have counsellor contacts available
- Maintain list of support organisations

2 Tips and Exercises to Save the Environment

Save Energy
Daily Tips

1. Turn off lights when leaving a room.
2. Unplug chargers when not in use.
3. Use natural light during the day.
4. Wear warmer clothes instead of turning up the heat.

Energy Audit Adventure

1. Create an 'energy checklist'.
2. Check each room for unused devices.
3. Count lights left on unnecessarily.
4. Make 'Switch Off' reminder cards.
5. Place cards near switches.

Solar Power Experiment

1. Place ice cubes in sun and shade.
2. Time how long they take to melt.
3. Record temperature differences.
4. Learn about solar energy.

No-Electricity Hour Challenge

1. Plan fun activities without electricity.
2. Read books using natural light.
3. Play board games.
4. Share stories with family.
5. Document energy saved.

Reduce & Recycle
Daily Tips

1. Use both sides of the paper when drawing.
2. Separate recyclables from trash.
3. Use a reusable lunch box and water bottle.
4. Give away toys you don't use anymore.

Recycling Sorting Station

1. Decorate boxes for different materials.
2. Label: Paper, Plastic, Glass, Metal.
3. Create picture guides for each box.
4. Track weekly recycling amounts.

Newspaper Pot Making

1. Fold newspaper into small pots.
2. Fill with soil.
3. Plant seeds.
4. Watch them grow.
5. Transfer to garden after the seeds have sprouted.

Eco-Art Project

1. Collect clean recyclable items.
2. Sort by colour and material.
3. Create artwork or useful items.
4. Display your creation.
5. Share recycling facts with viewers.

Plant Your Own Seeds

Plant seeds and watch them grow.

Create a bird feeder from recycled materials.

Pick up litter (with gloves!).

Start a small garden or plant herbs.

Build a Bug Hotel

1. Collect sticks, leaves, and bark.
2. Find a safe outdoor spot.
3. Stack materials in layers.
4. Add hollow stems and pine cones.
5. Observe daily visitors.

Butterfly Garden Project

1. Research butterfly-friendly plants.
2. Plant nectar-rich flowers.
3. Create a water source.
4. Keep a butterfly diary.
5. Take photos of visitors.

Composting Adventure

1. Set up a compost bin with the help of an adult.
2. Collect fruit/vegetable scraps.
3. Add dry leaves and paper.
4. Monitor temperature weekly.
5. Use compost for plants

3 FOOD WASTE WARRIORS

Daily Tips
1. Take only what you can eat.
2. Store leftovers properly.
3. Learn about food expiration dates.
4. Help plan meals to avoid waste.

Kitchen Scrap Garden

1. Save seeds from fruits and vegetables
2. Regrow celery/lettuce bottoms in water
3. Plant sprouted potatoes
4. Document growth progress

Food Waste Monitor

1. Create a weekly chart
2. Record uneaten food
3. Measure waste reduction
4. Suggest improvements
5. Share tips with friends

Remember

Take pictures of your activities to create an eco-diary. Share your achievements with friends and family. Every small action helps protect our planet.

4 Tips for Teaching Children Respect for Diversity and Equality

Teaching children to respect religious differences and avoid discrimination based on caste, class, or gender is an essential step in fostering empathy, understanding, and social harmony. Here are some practical tips:

1. **Model Respectful Behaviour**

    Be an Example: Children learn by observing adults. Show respect for diverse religions, cultures, and individuals.

    Use Inclusive Language: Speak positively about all groups and avoid stereotypes or derogatory remarks.

2. **Educate About Diversity**

    Expose Them to Different Cultures and Religions: Share stories, celebrate festivals, or visit places of worship of different religions to promote understanding.

    Encourage Questions: Allow children to ask questions about differences and answer them in a positive and non-judgemental way.

3. **Promote Empathy**

    Use Stories and Role-Playing: Read books and share stories that highlight the importance of respect and empathy. Role-play situations where they can practice putting themselves in others' shoes.

Discuss Feelings: Talk about how discrimination or exclusion makes people feel.

4. **Teach Universal Values**

   Emphasise Kindness and Fairness: Explain why fairness and kindness are better than prejudice.

   Highlight Common Humanity: Teach that, despite differences, all people have the same basic needs, emotions, and rights.

5. **Address Bias Early**

   Challenge Stereotypes: When children express biased views, gently correct them and explain why they are inaccurate or unfair.

   Encourage Critical Thinking: Help them understand how biases form and why they should question them.

6. **Encourage Inclusive Friendships**

   Promote Diverse Social Interactions: Arrange playdates and activities with children from varied backgrounds.

   Value Differences: Highlight how diversity makes life more interesting and rich.

7. **Address Media and Social Influences**

   Monitor Media Content: Ensure the media they consume portrays diverse groups respectfully.

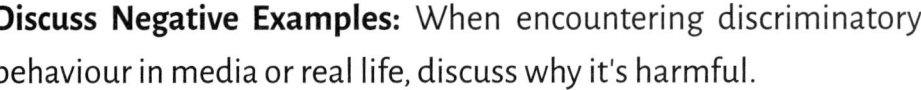

Discuss Negative Examples: When encountering discriminatory behaviour in media or real life, discuss why it's harmful.

8. **Celebrate Gender Equality**

   Avoid Gender Roles: Encourage boys and girls equally to explore interests and responsibilities.

   Showcase Role Models: Highlight diverse role models who broke stereotypes in various fields.

9. **Engage in Community Service**

   Volunteer Together: Participate in activities like helping the less fortunate, which can develop empathy and a sense of equality.

   Discuss Inequalities: Use these experiences to talk about systemic injustices and the importance of fairness.

10. **Create an Open Environment**

    Encourage Conversations: Let children express their observations and feelings openly.

    Validate and Guide: Praise their respect and fairness, and guide them when they make mistakes.

5 Exercises to Promote Cleanliness in Kids

1. **Daily Clean-Up Routine**
   - **Morning and Evening Tasks:** Assign simple tasks like making their bed in the morning and tidying up their toys or books before bedtime.

   - **Set a Timer:** Make it a game by setting a timer for a quick clean-up session (eg., "Let's tidy up in 10 minutes!").

2. **Sorting and Organising**
   - **Toy Sorting Game:** Encourage them to sort toys into categories like cars, dolls, or blocks.

   - **Colour-Coded Organisation:** Use bins or boxes with specific colours for different items (eg., red for books, blue for toys).

   - **Pick up Litter:** Turn it into a fun activity by asking them to pick up litter around the house or yard and dispose of it in the trash.

   - **Recycling Game:** Teach them about recycling by having them sort trash into bins for paper, plastic, and metal.

4. **Decluttering Challenges**
   - **One-In-One-Out Rule:** For every new item they bring into their room, have them remove an old one they no longer use.
   - **Five-Minute Declutter:** Each day, spend five minutes together putting away items where they belong.

   ### 5. Personalised Cleaning Zones

   - **Assign Zones:** Divide spaces like their room or a shared area into zones and make them responsible for keeping their zone tidy.
   - **Reward Progress:** Offer small rewards or praise when their zone is clean and organised.

6. **Fun Cleaning Tools**
   - **Mini Cleaning Supplies:** Give them child-sized brooms, dustpans, or cleaning cloths to make cleaning feel like play.
   - **Decorated Bins:** Let them decorate their storage bins or baskets to take ownership of keeping things organised.

7. **Cleaning Songs and Dance**
   - **Music Motivation:** Play their favourite songs while cleaning to make it enjoyable.
   - **Dance and Clean:** Combine cleaning with dancing—sweep the floor with dance moves!

8. **Outdoor Clean-Up**
   - **Gardening:** Teach them to pick up leaves, pull weeds, or water plants to maintain outdoor spaces.
   - **Playground Cleaning:** Organise a mini cleanup drive at the playground or park with friends.

9. **Visual Checklists**
   - **Use Pictures:** Create a visual checklist with pictures showing what a clean room should look like.
   - **Star Chart:** Track their cleaning efforts with stickers or stars and celebrate milestones.

10. **Story-Based Cleaning**
    - **Tidy-Up Tales:** Create a story where the hero cleans up to save the day.
    - **Clean-Up Adventures:** Pretend they are explorers or detectives finding "lost treasures" while organising.
    - **Bonus:** Include Educational Messages.

Appendix

A short note about the people who formed the Indian Constitution:

Dr B R Ambedkar (1891-1956)

Born into a low-caste family, Ambedkar faced many hardships but went on to become highly educated, studying at Columbia University and the London School of Economics. He fought against untouchability and worked for equal rights. As Chairman of the Constitution's Drafting Committee, he played the biggest role in writing India's Constitution. He also served as India's first Law Minister. He is known as the "Father of Indian Constitution" and spent his life fighting for the rights of oppressed people. He converted to Buddhism and inspired millions to follow his path.

N Gopalaswami Ayyangar (1882-1953)

A very skilled administrator and politician who served in many important positions. Before India became independent, he was Prime Minister of Kashmir and also worked as a senior government officer in Madras (now Chennai). He was great at writing laws and helped decide how India's railways and defense would work. After independence, he became a minister in India's first government and helped handle the Kashmir situation.

Alladi Krishnaswami Ayyar (1883-1953)

One of India's greatest legal minds of his time. He started as a lawyer in Madras and became so good that people called him the "Law's Encyclopaedia." He could remember complicated laws without looking at books! While helping to write the Constitution, he made sure the legal language was perfect and helped explain difficult legal ideas in simple ways. He was especially good at figuring out how to divide powers between the center and states.

Dr K M Munshi (1887-1971)

A lawyer who was also a famous writer and educator. He wrote many books in English and Gujarati and started the Bharatiya Vidya Bhavan, a major educational institution. During the freedom movement, he worked closely with Mahatma Gandhi. While helping write the Constitution, he focused on protecting India's culture and languages. He also helped convince many princely states to join India. Later, he served as Governor and helped establish many educational institutions.

Syed Mohammad Saadulla (1885-1955)

A prominent Muslim leader from Assam who served as the Prime Minister of Assam multiple times before Independence. He was highly educated and understood both Islamic and modern laws. In the Constituent Assembly, he made sure that minority rights were protected and helped bridge understanding between different communities. He was known for being very thoughtful and fair in his approach to complex issues.

N Madhava Rau (1887-1972)

He replaced B L Mitter on the drafting committee. Before this, he served as Prime Minister of Mysore state and was known for being a very honest administrator. He had deep knowledge of how governments work and helped write parts of the Constitution dealing with state administration. He was especially good at explaining complicated ideas in simple language.

T T Krishnamachari (1899-1974)

He joined the drafting committee after D P Khaitan passed away. He was both a successful businessman and a skilled politician. Later, he became India's Finance Minister twice. While working on the Constitution, he helped write the parts about India's economy and financial system. He was known for speaking his mind and suggesting practical solutions to problems.

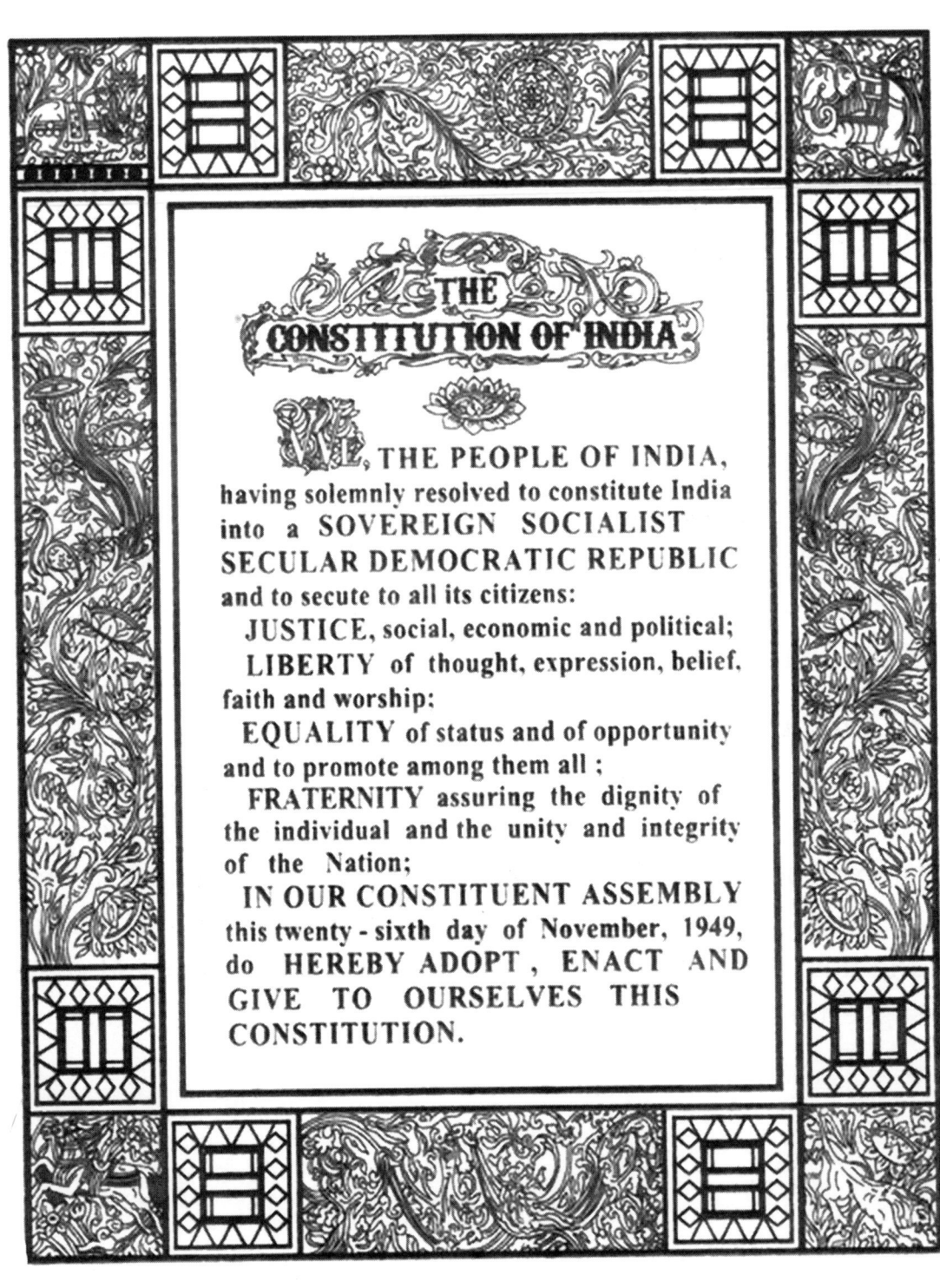

THE CONSTITUTION OF INDIA

WE, THE PEOPLE OF INDIA, having solemnly resolved to constitute India into a SOVEREIGN SOCIALIST SECULAR DEMOCRATIC REPUBLIC and to secute to all its citizens:

JUSTICE, social, economic and political;

LIBERTY of thought, expression, belief, faith and worship;

EQUALITY of status and of opportunity and to promote among them all ;

FRATERNITY assuring the dignity of the individual and the unity and integrity of the Nation;

IN OUR CONSTITUENT ASSEMBLY this twenty - sixth day of November, 1949, do HEREBY ADOPT, ENACT AND GIVE TO OURSELVES THIS CONSTITUTION.

Glossary

Inculcates: To teach something repeatedly so it sticks in your mind, like when your parents keep reminding you to say "please" and "thank you" until it becomes a habit.

Futile: When something you try to do has no chance of working, like trying to fill a bucket that has a big hole in the bottom. It means your effort won't get you anywhere!

Persuade: To convince someone to do something or believe something by giving them good reasons.

Adhere: To stick to something or follow something closely.

Bestowed: To give something special to someone, like when a fairy godmother gives Cinderella her magical dress. It often means giving a gift or honour in a special way.

Leering: Looking at someone in a mean or creepy way that makes them feel uncomfortable. Think of a cartoon villain who gives that sneaky sideways look when planning something bad.

Ascertain: To find out something for sure, like being a detective and gathering clues until you know exactly what happened. It means making sure you have the right information.

Eradicate: To completely get rid of something, like when you clean your room so well that there's not a single speck of dirt left. It means making something disappear entirely.

Exhilarated: Feeling super excited and happy, like when you're on a roller coaster or when you just won your first game. It's that bubbly, thrilling feeling that makes you want to jump up and down.

Revelation: When you suddenly discover or learn something exciting that you didn't know before—like finding out there's going to be a surprise party for you! It's that "aha!" moment.